Coloring Book

CHRISTMAS

First Edition

Distributed by : CreateSpace

ISBN-13: 978-1540316295

ISBN-10: 1540316297

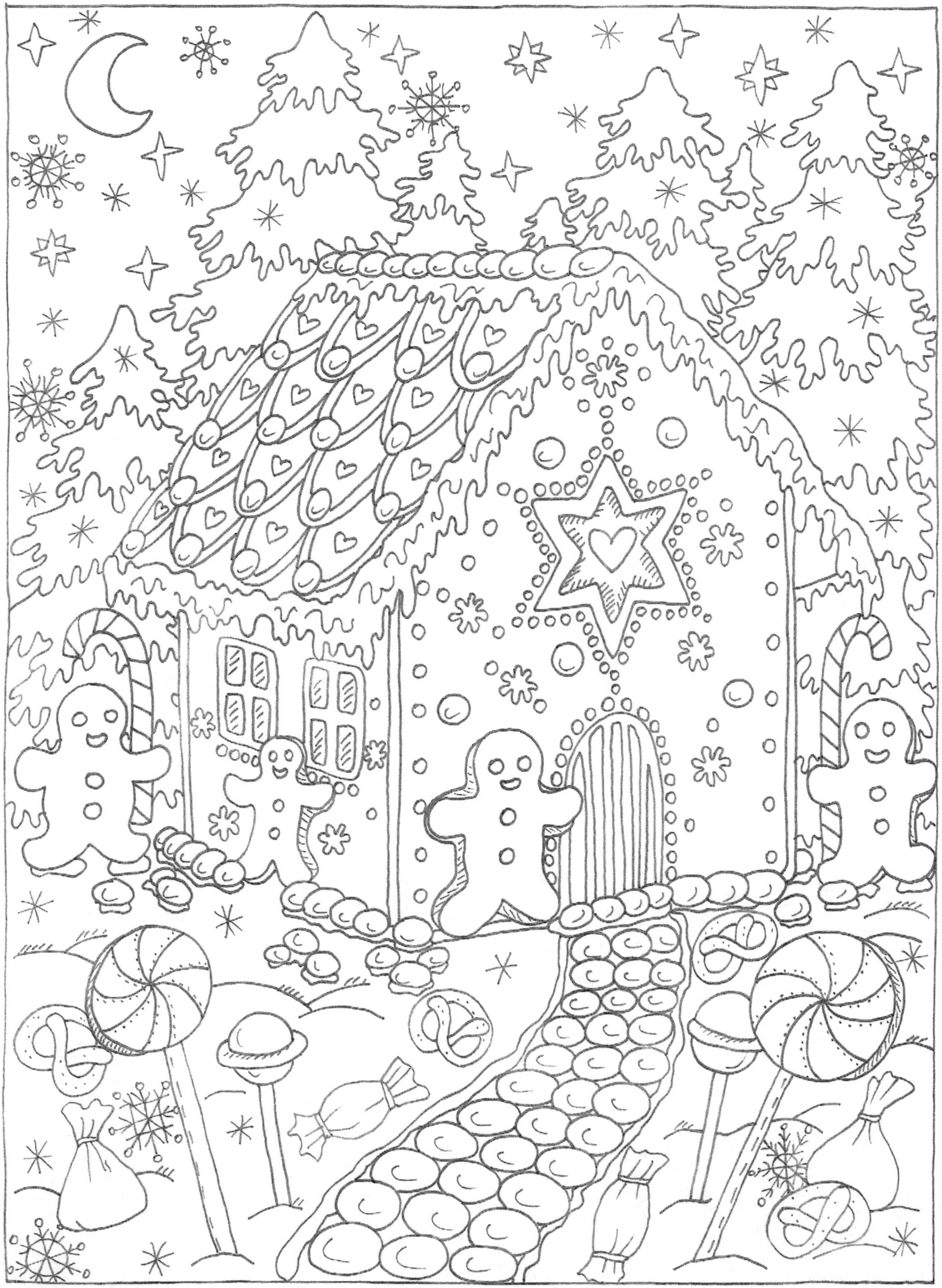

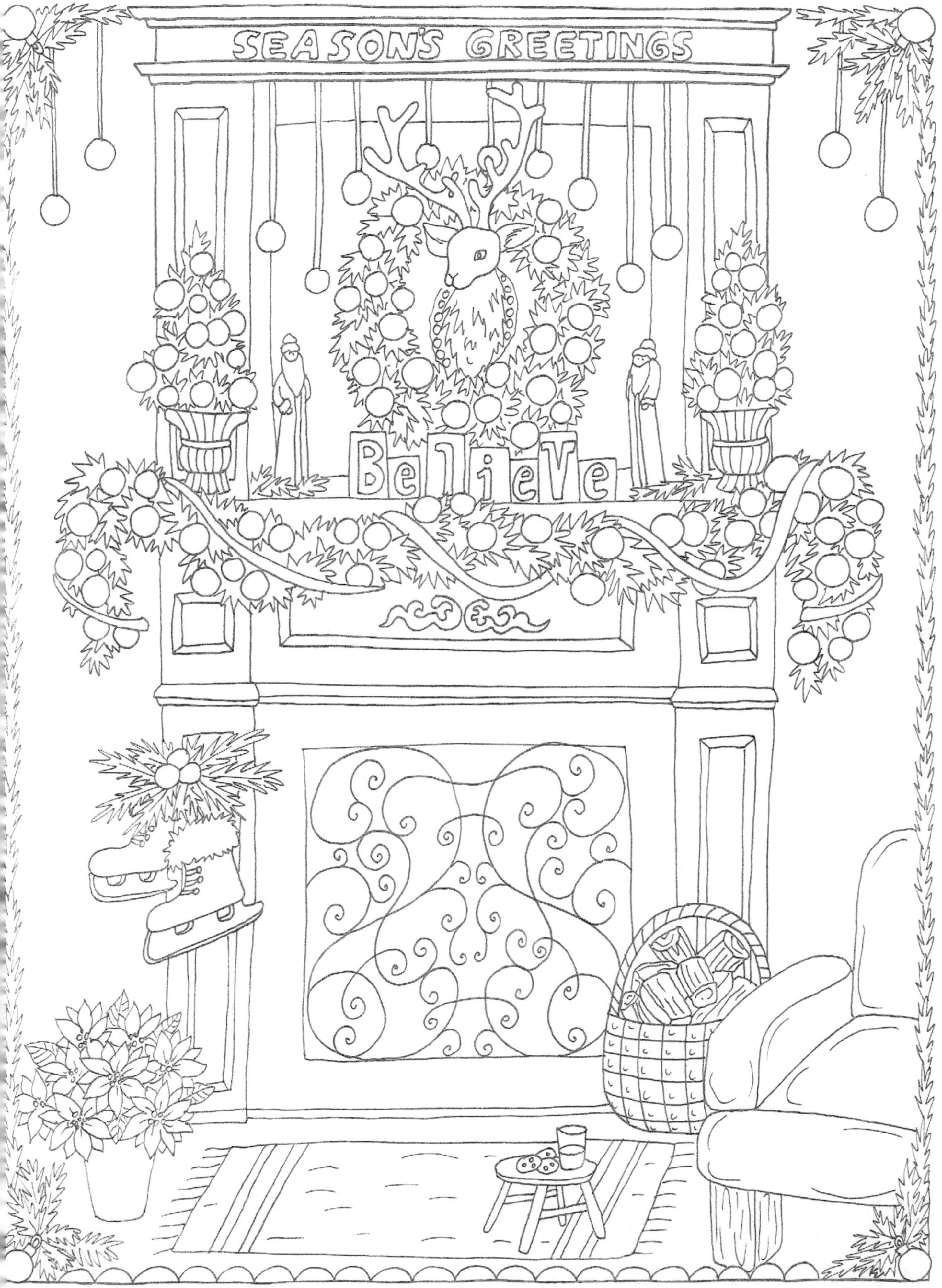
SEASON'S GREETINGS
BelieVe

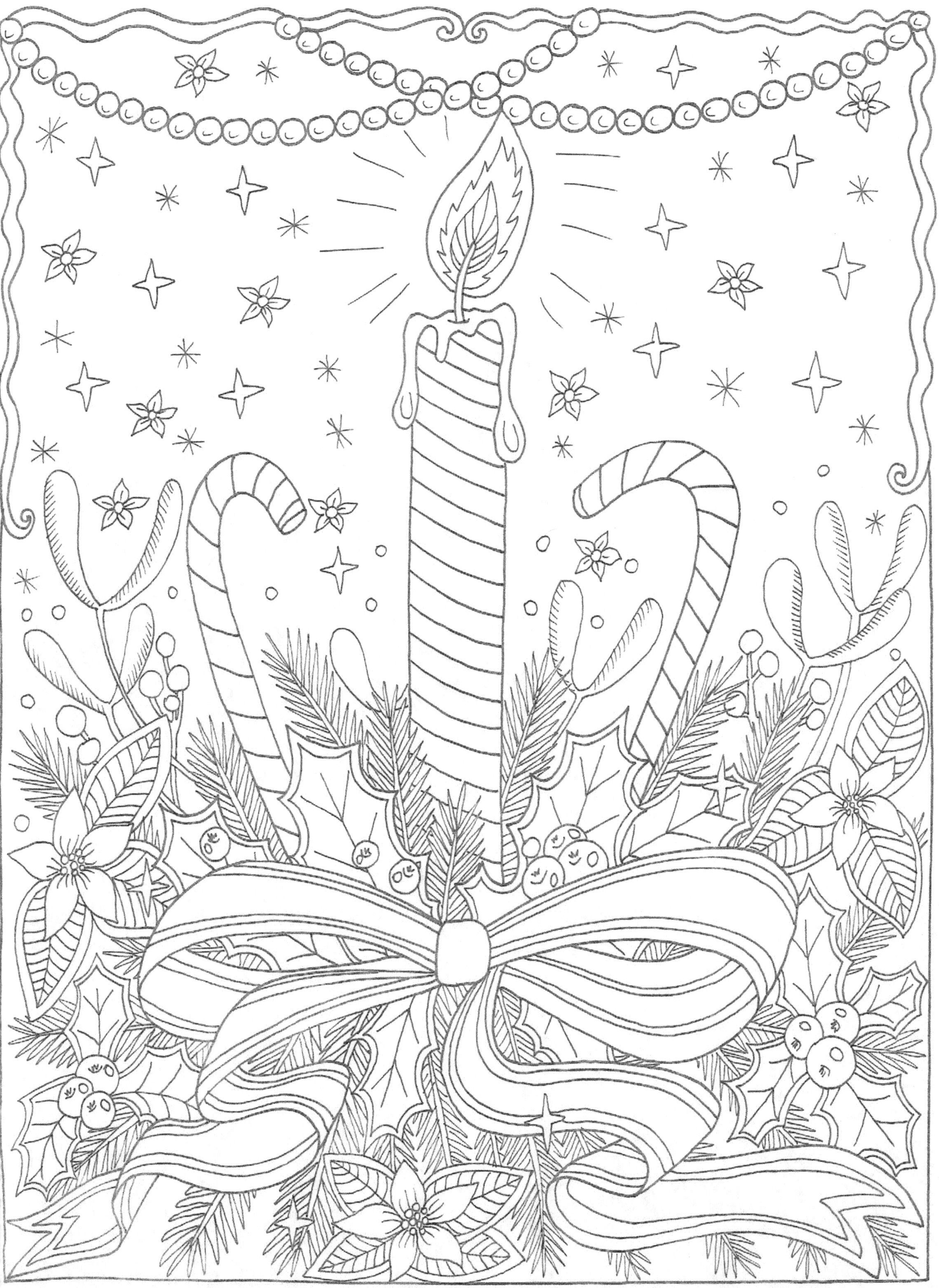

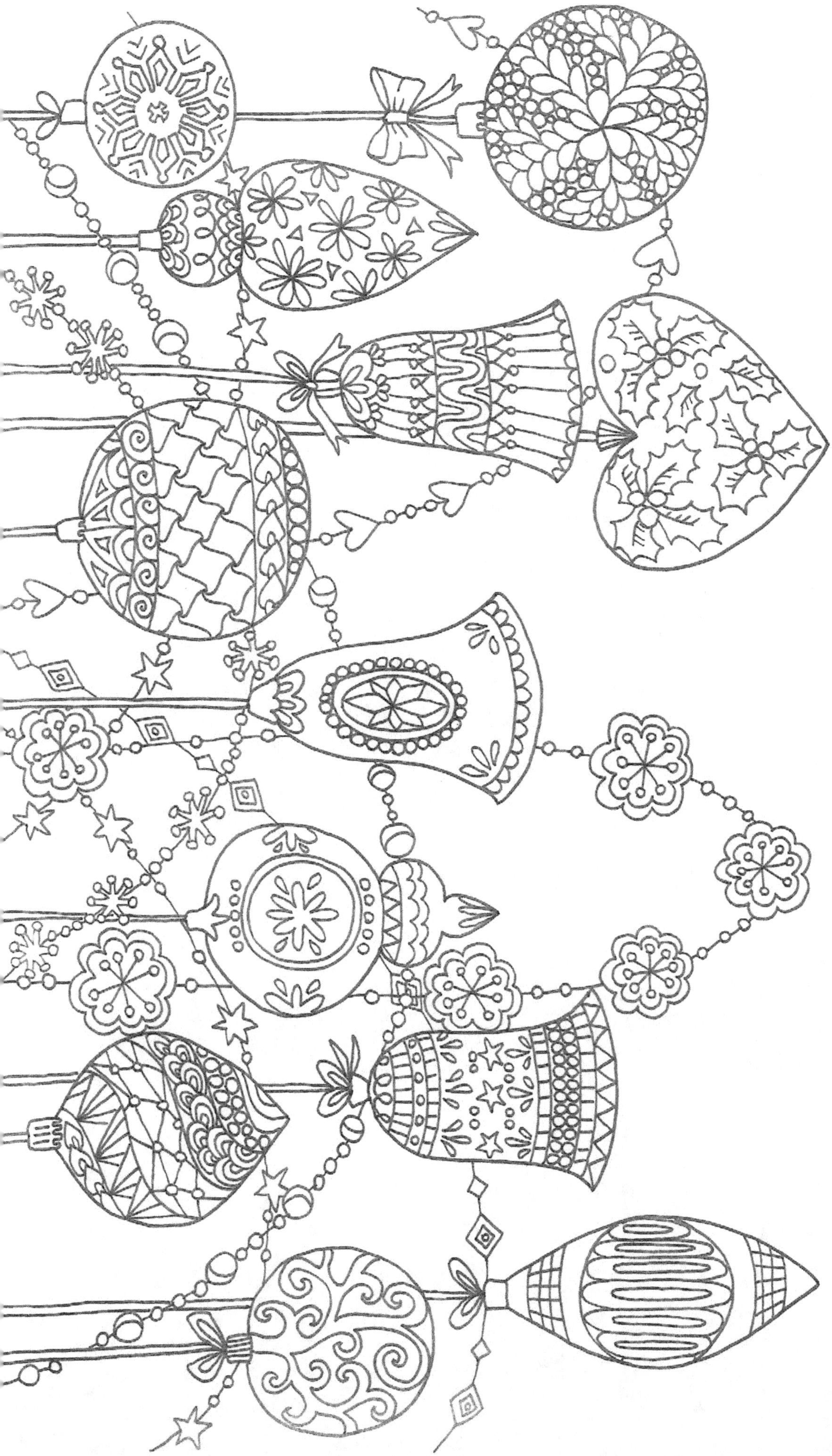

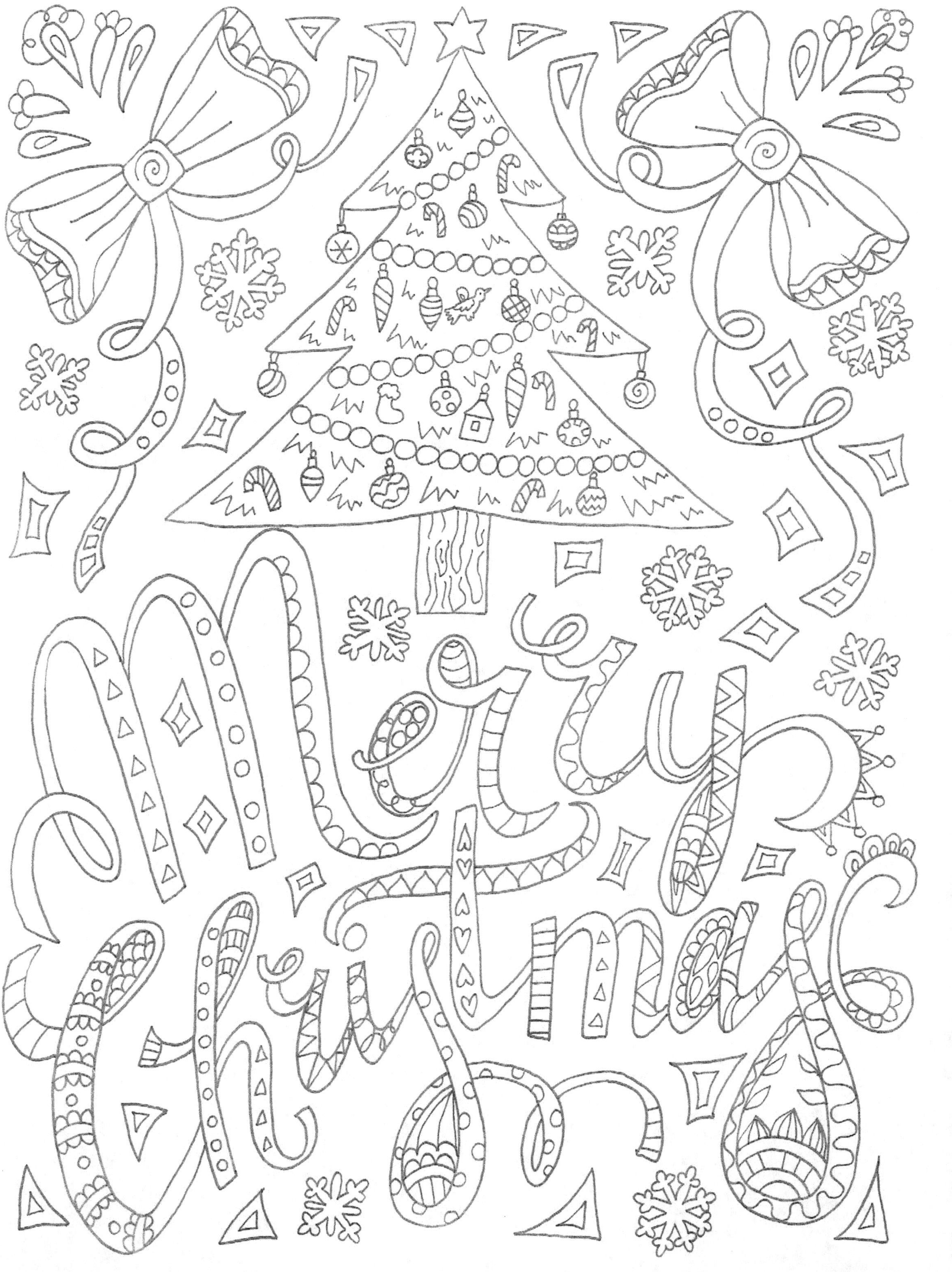
Merry Christmas

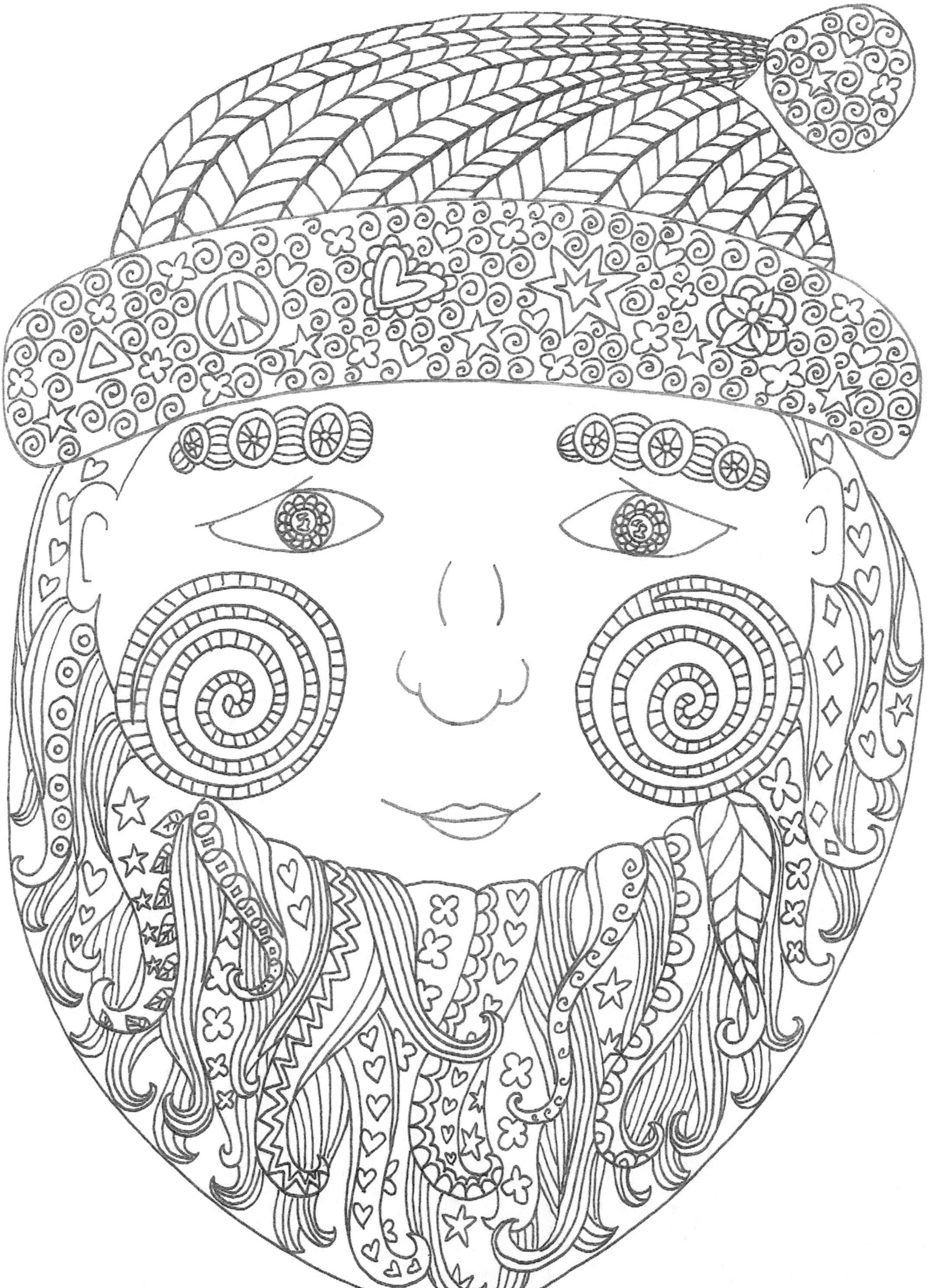

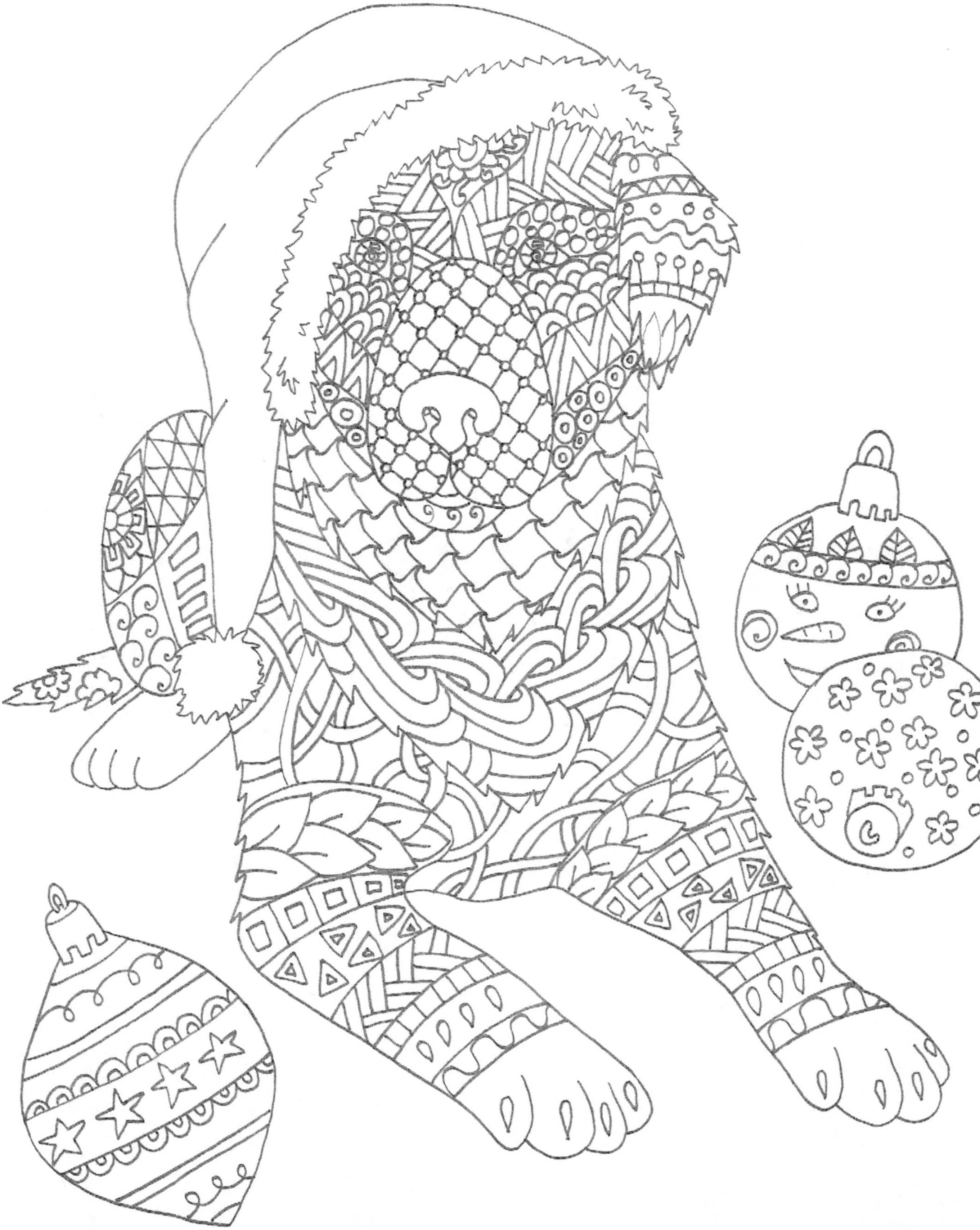

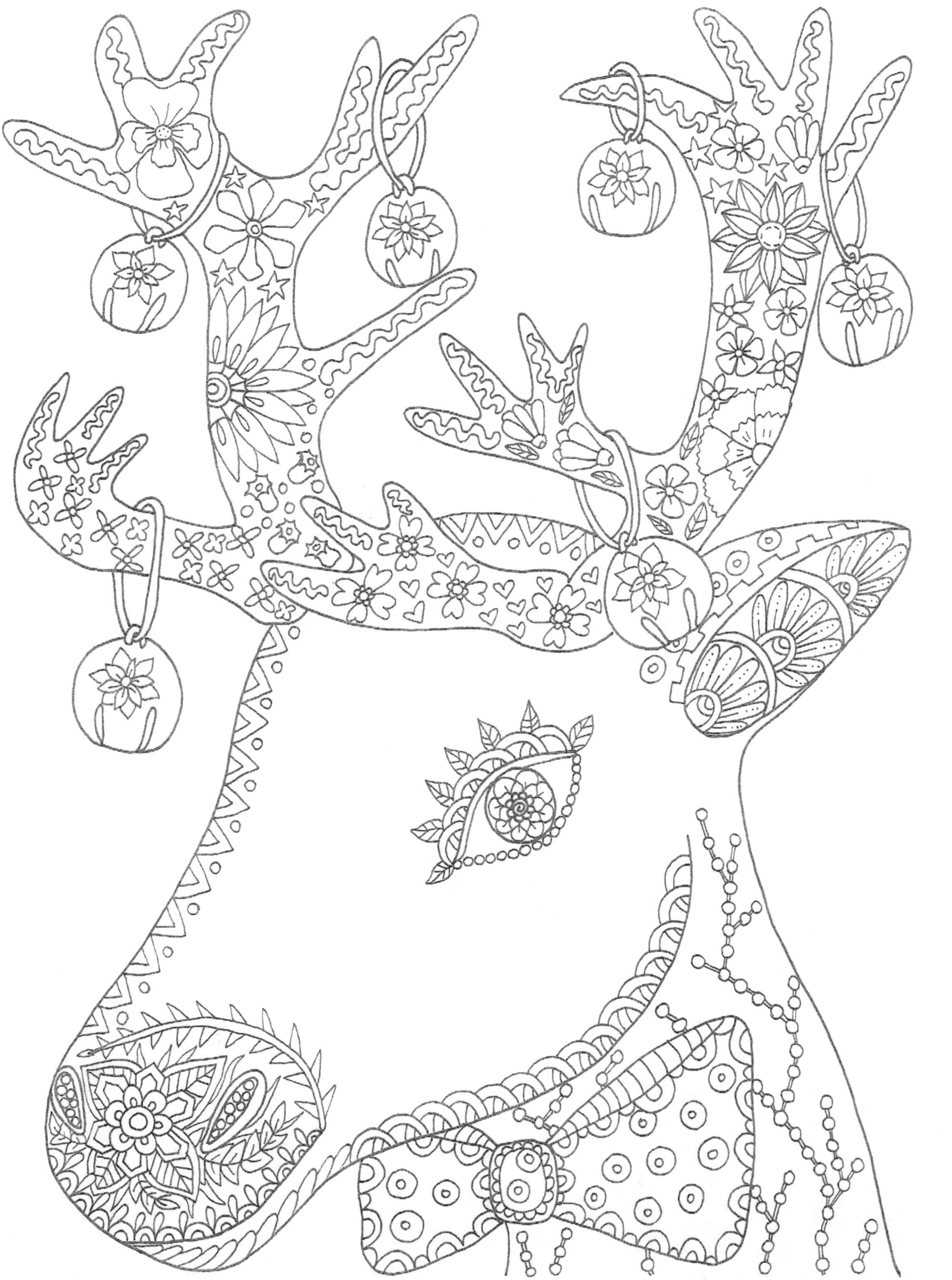

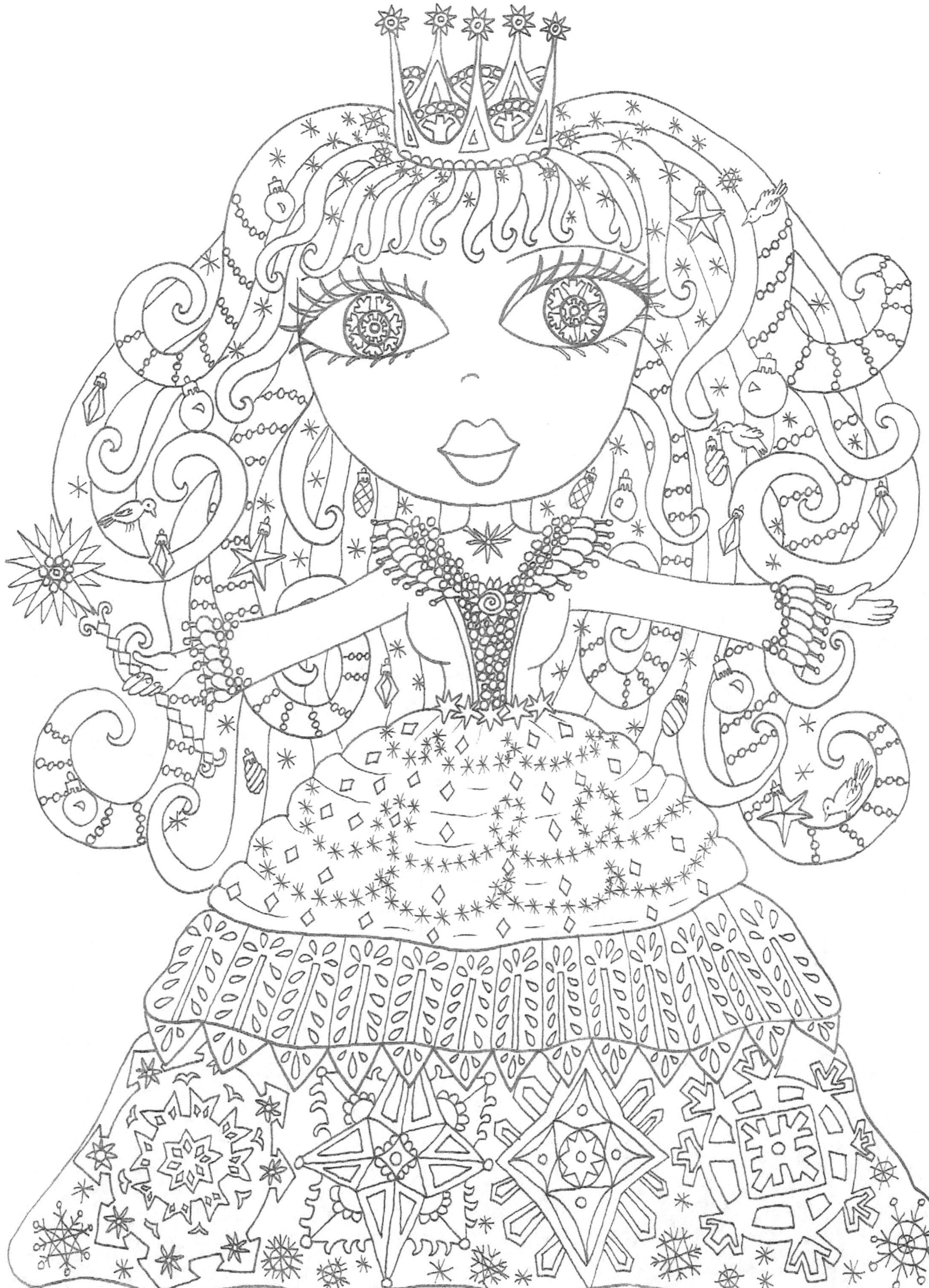

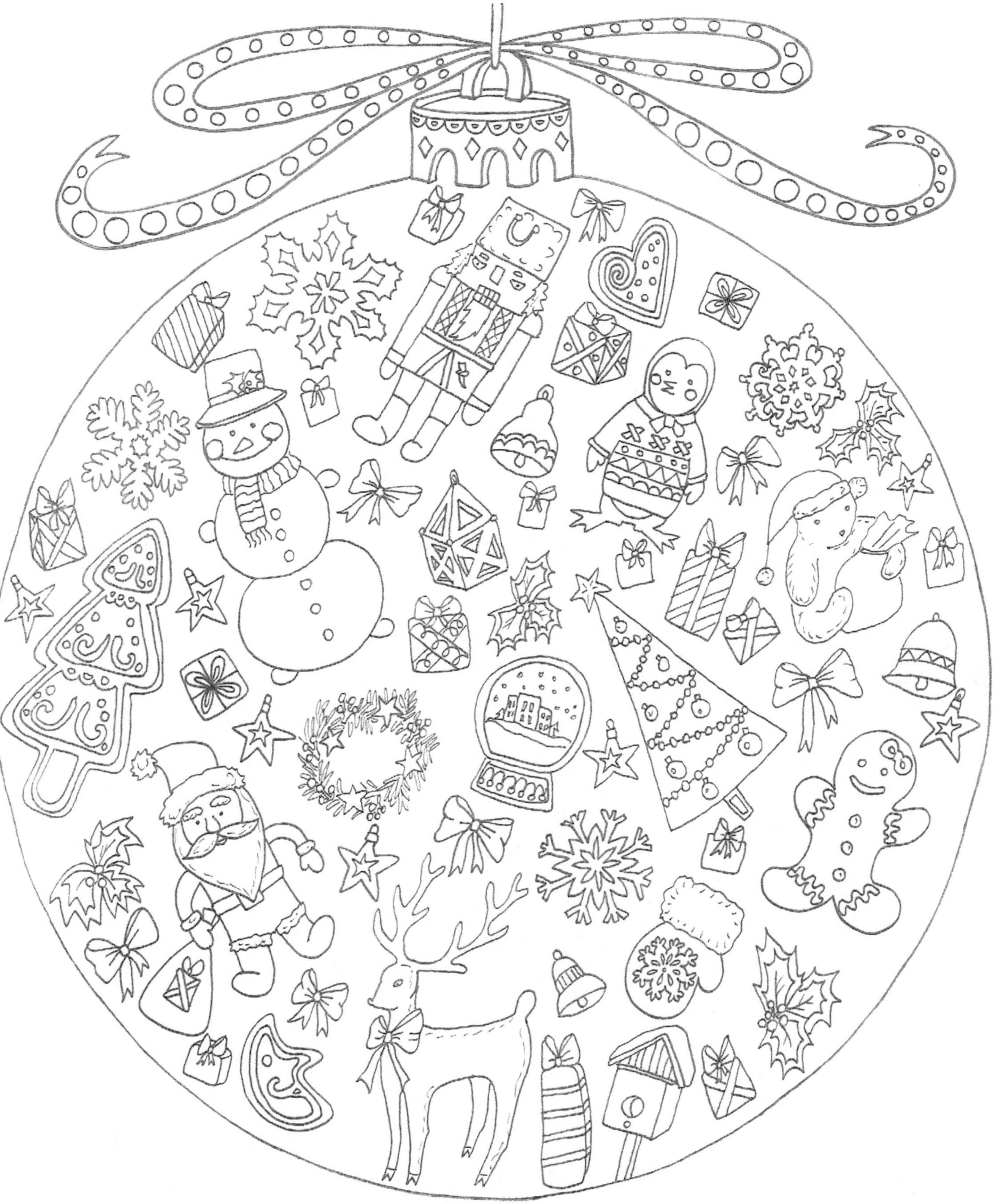

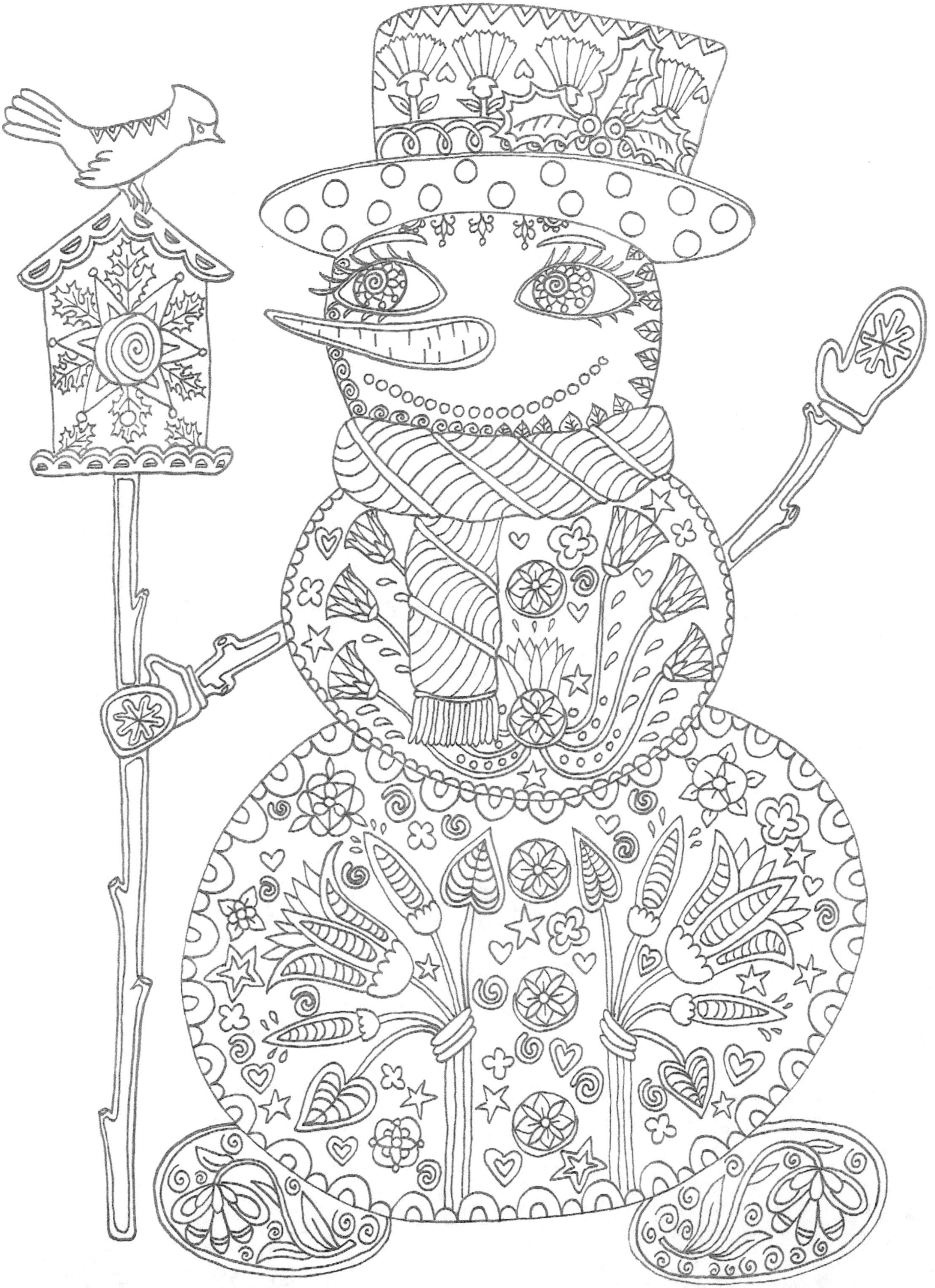

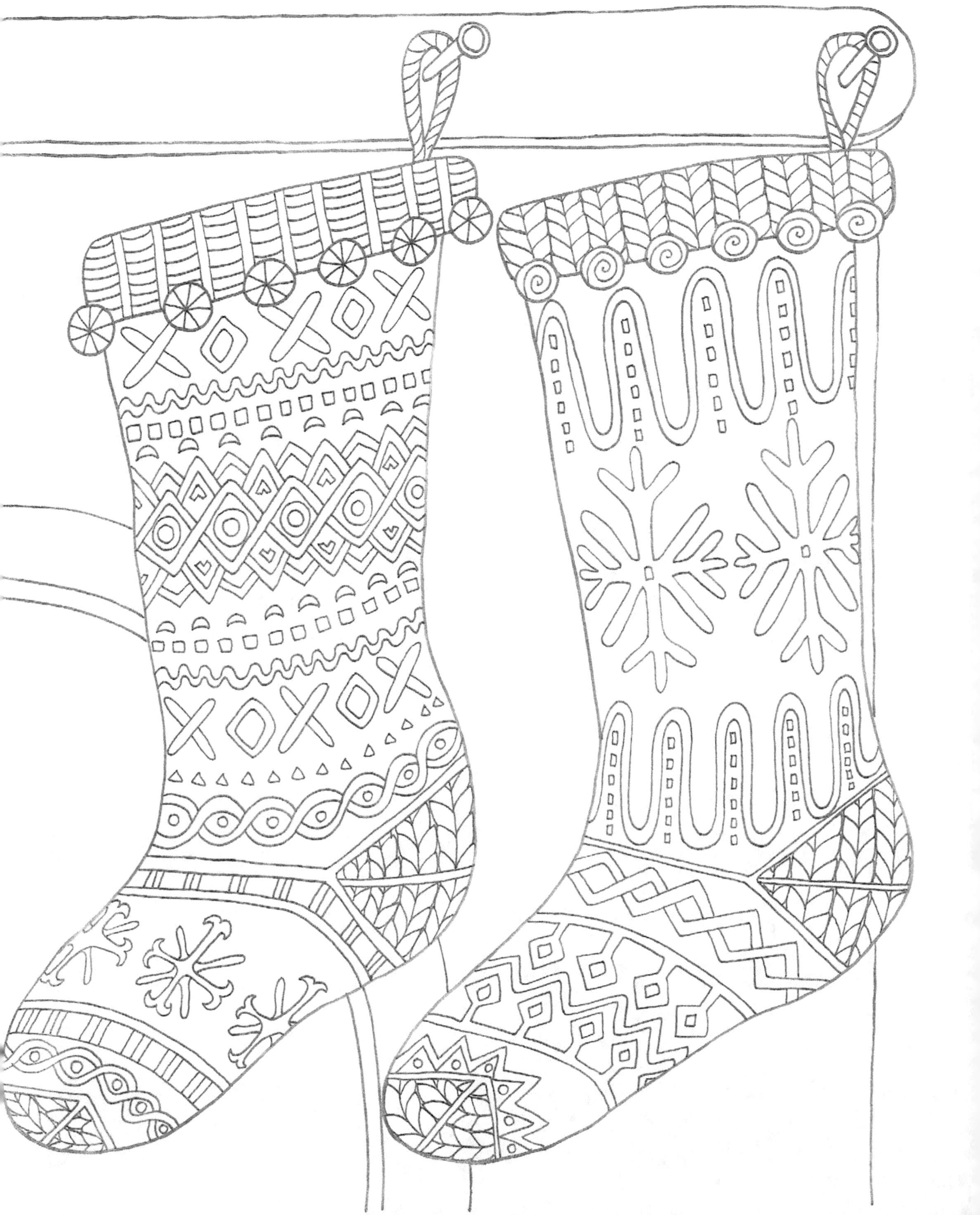

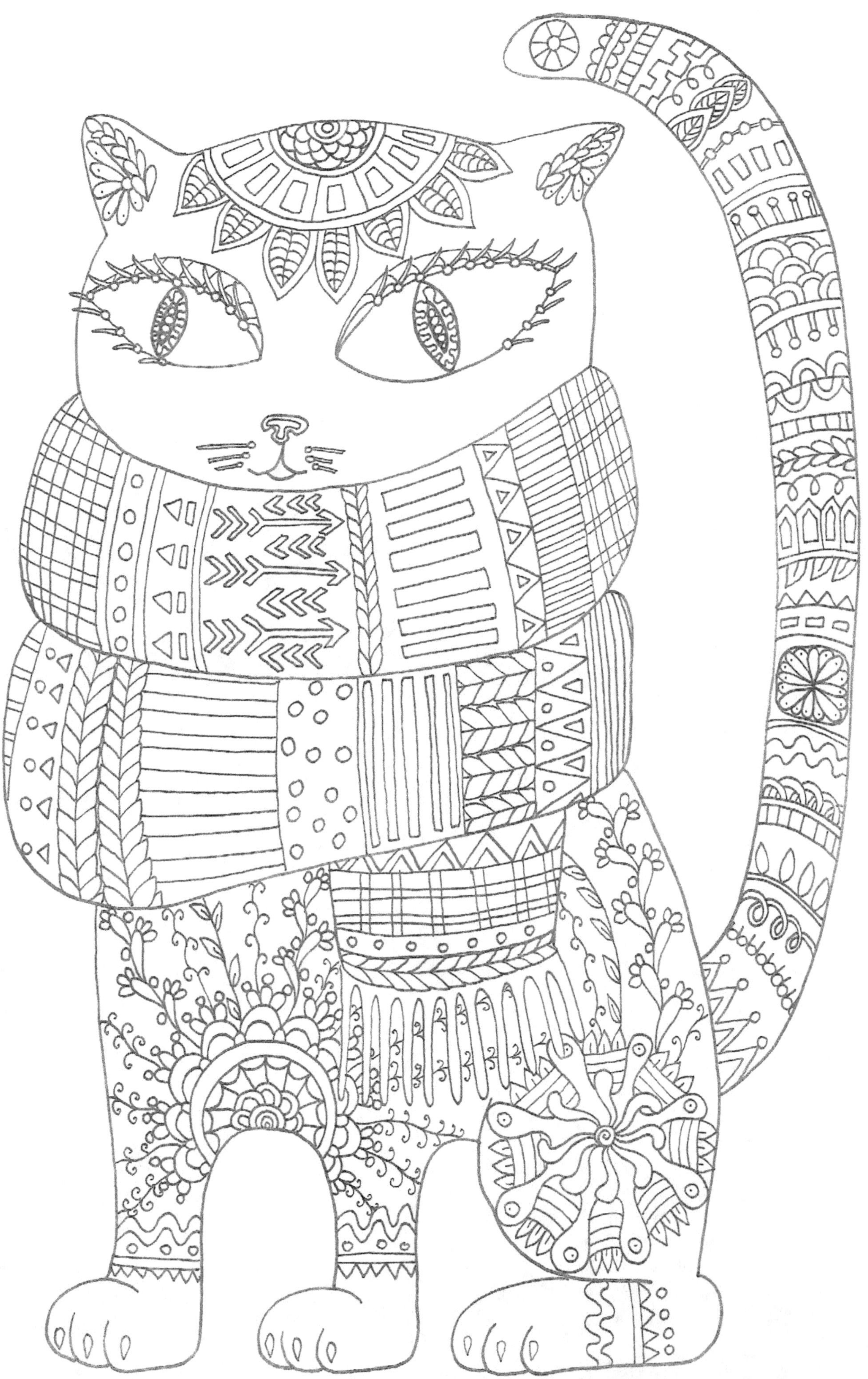

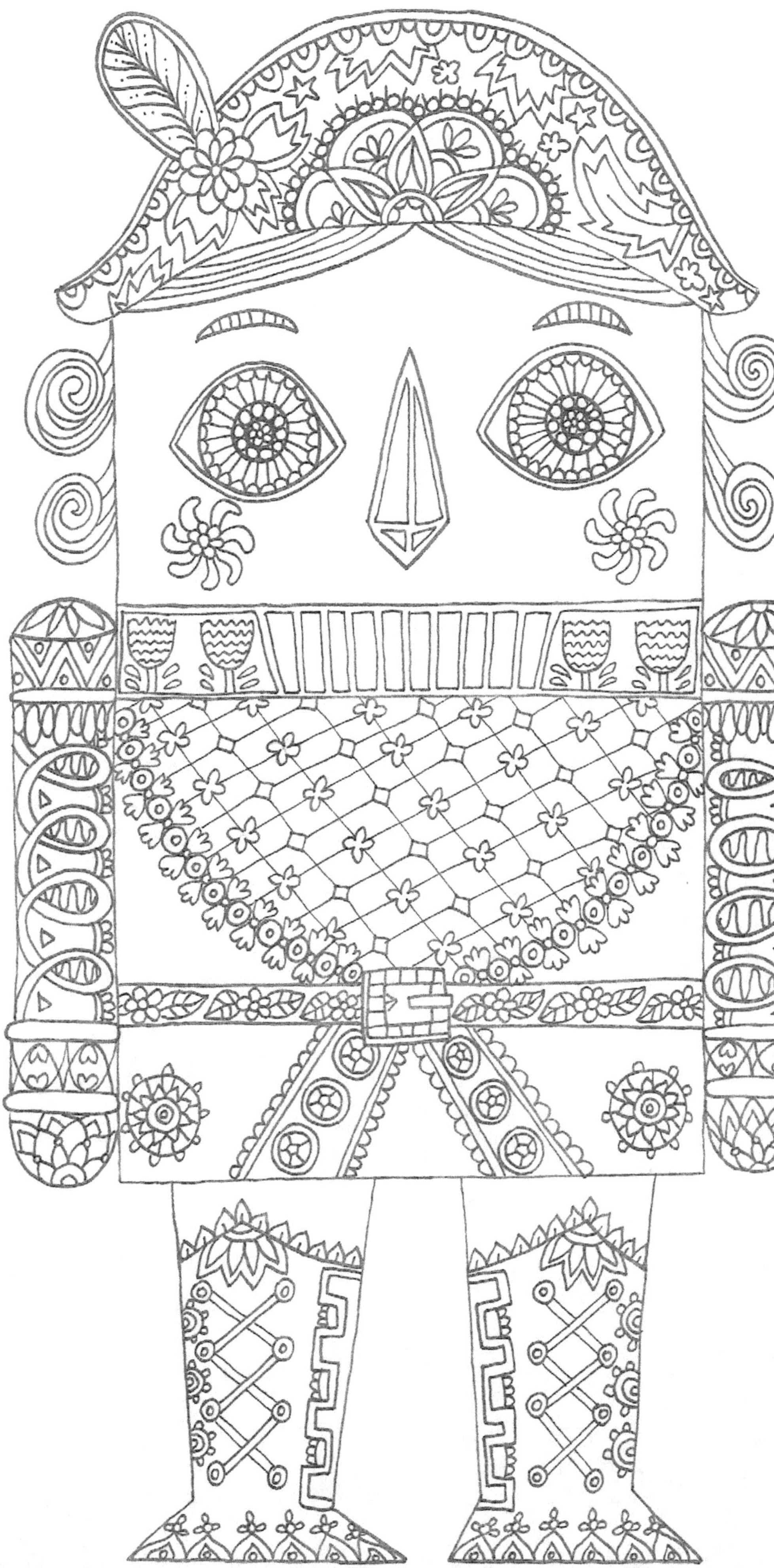

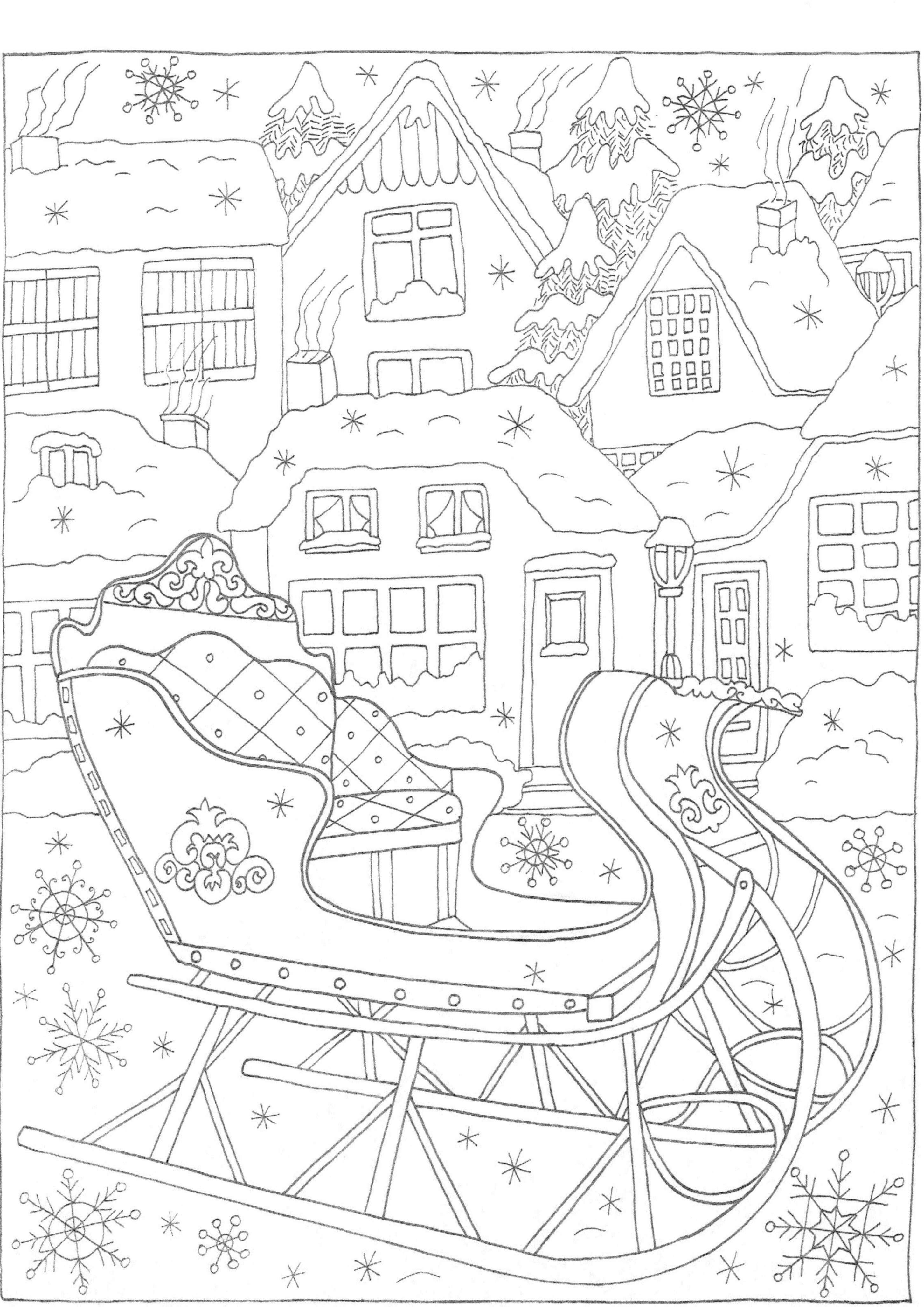

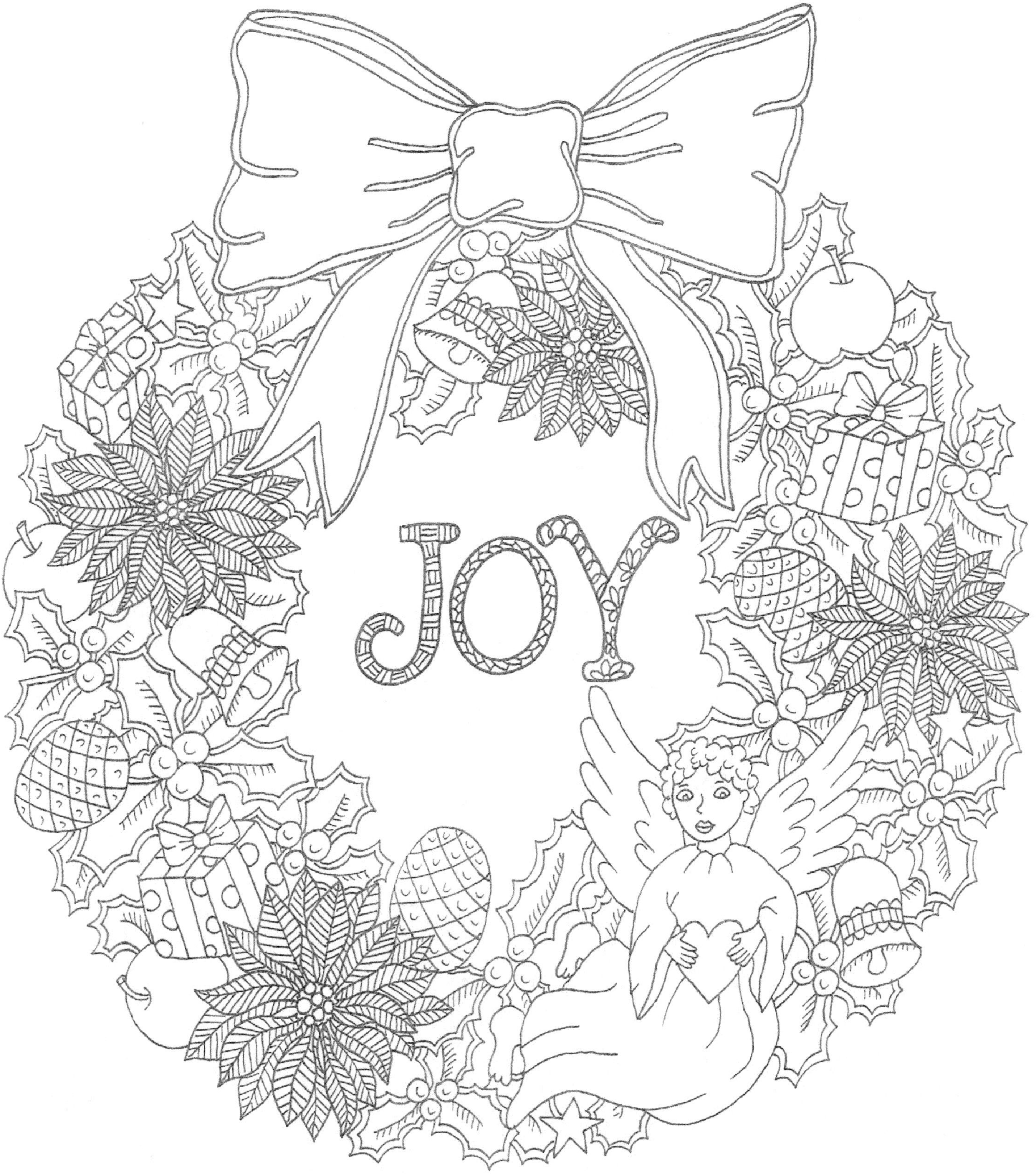
JOY

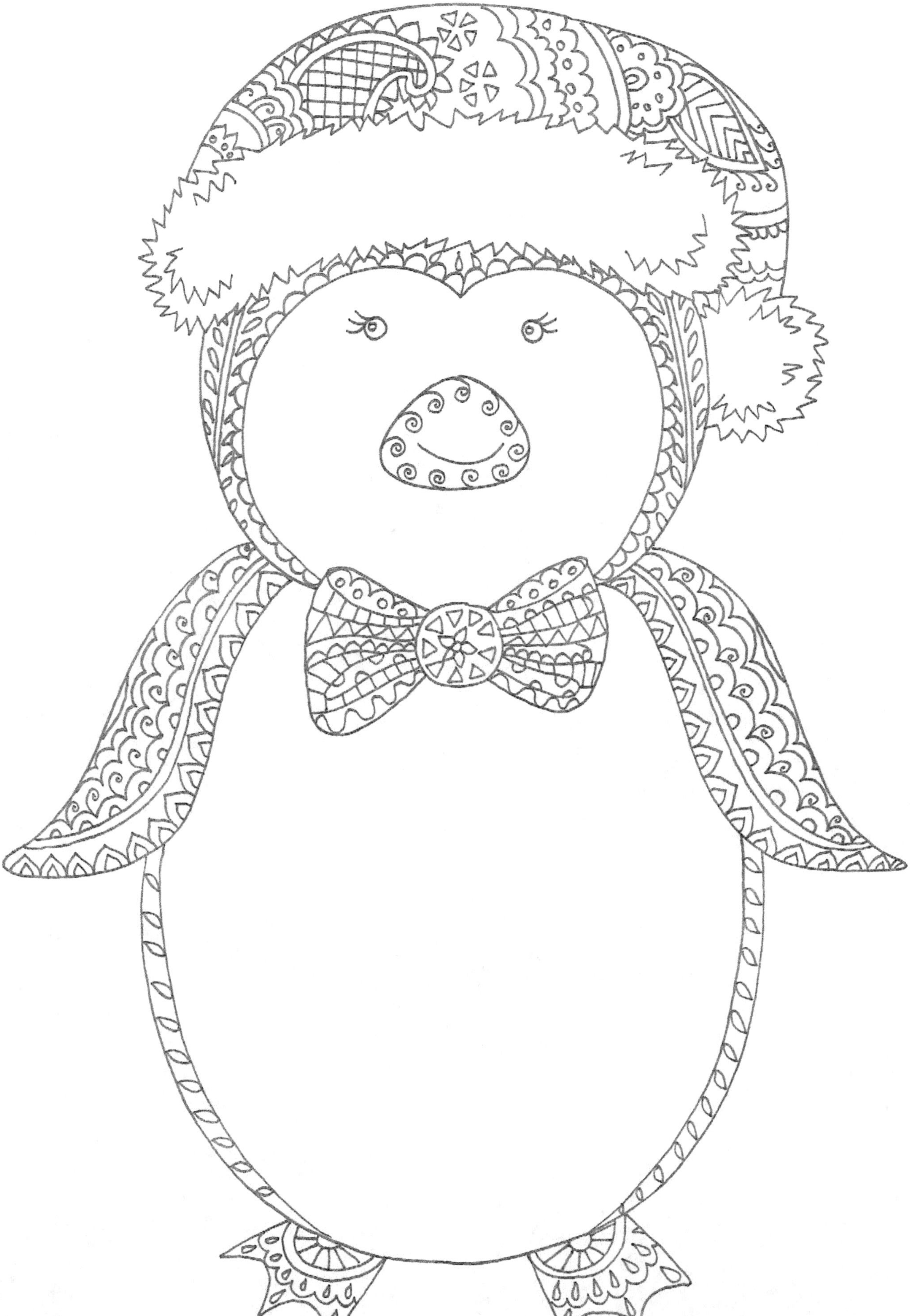

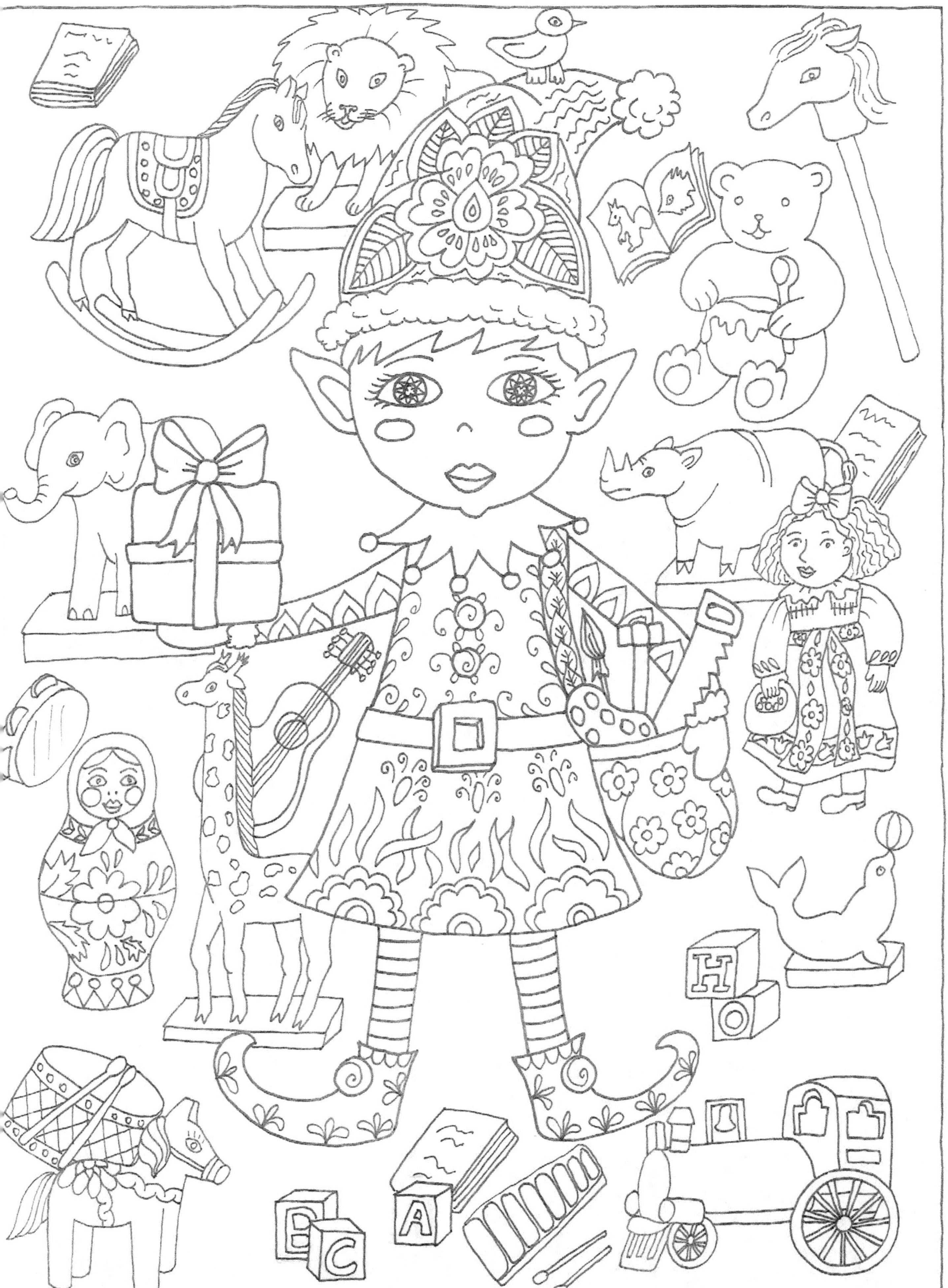
H
O
B
C
A

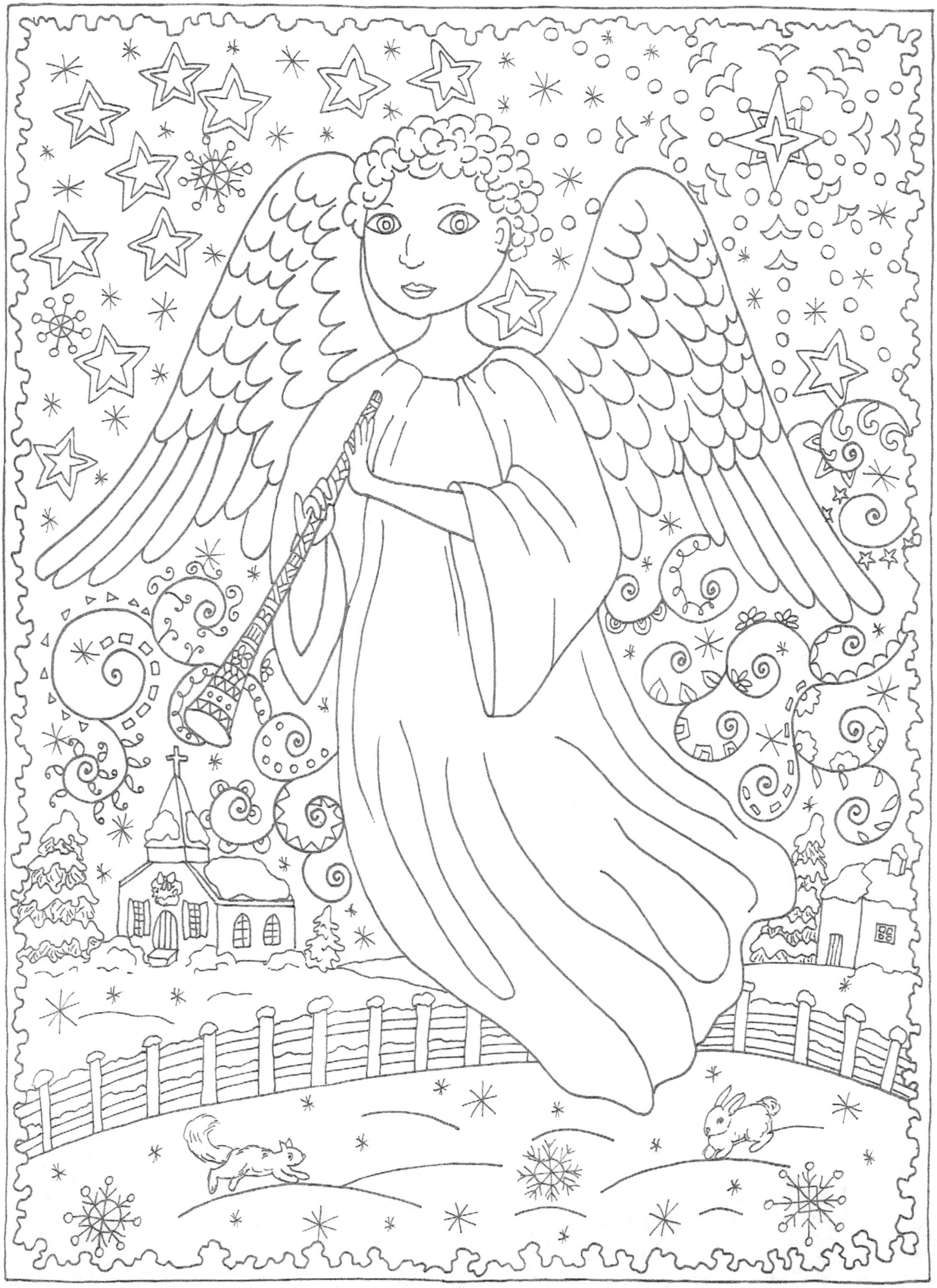

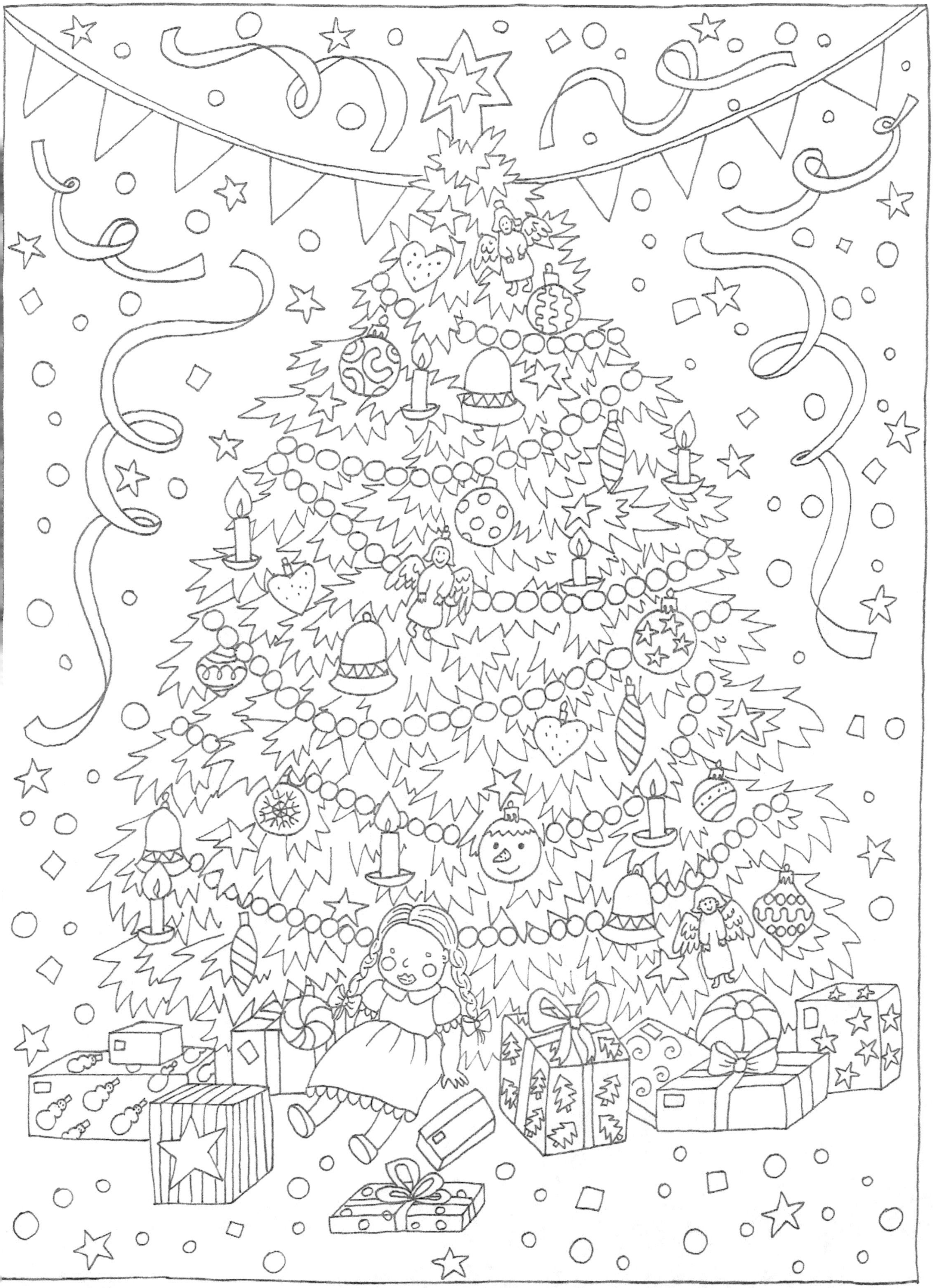

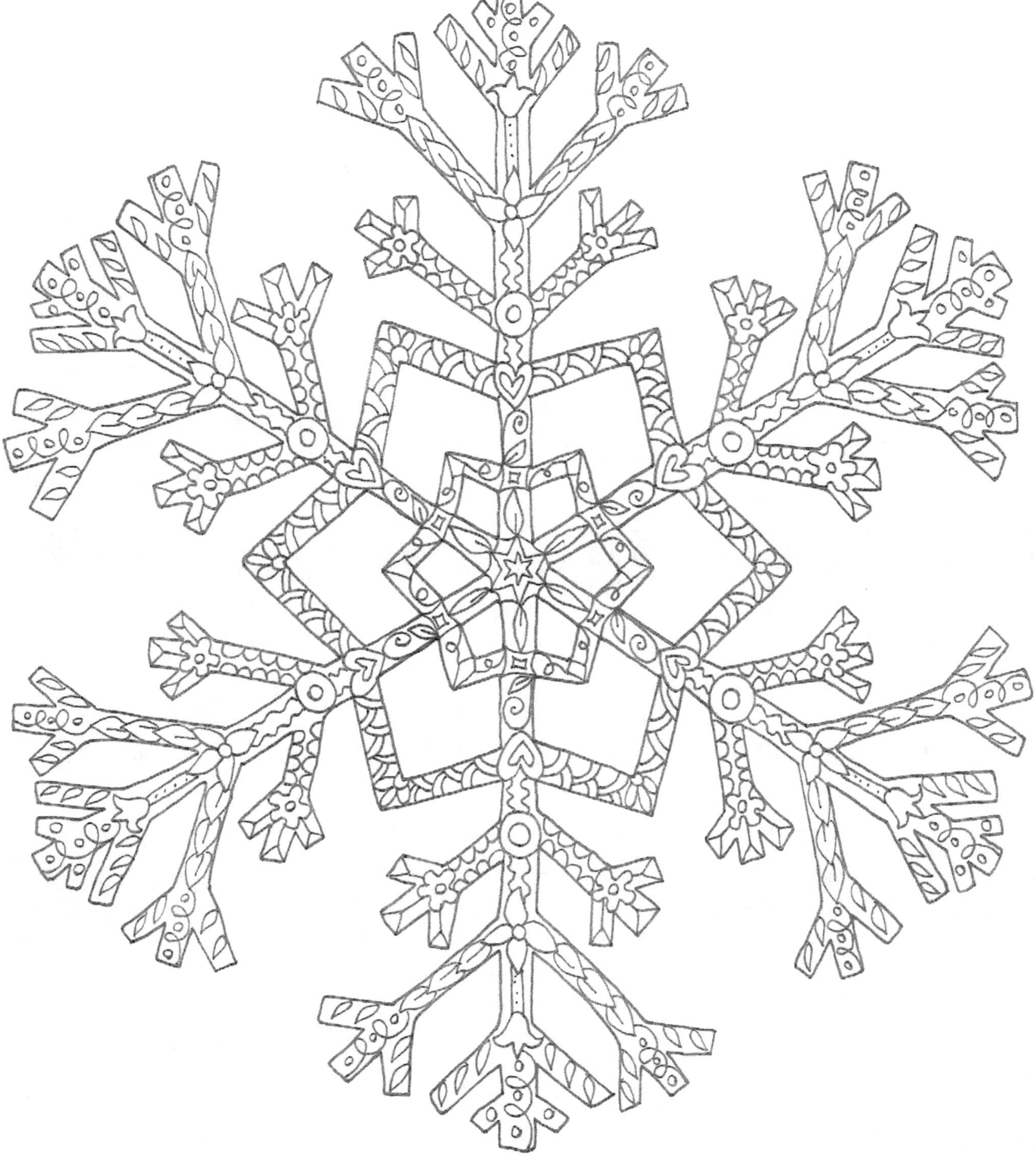

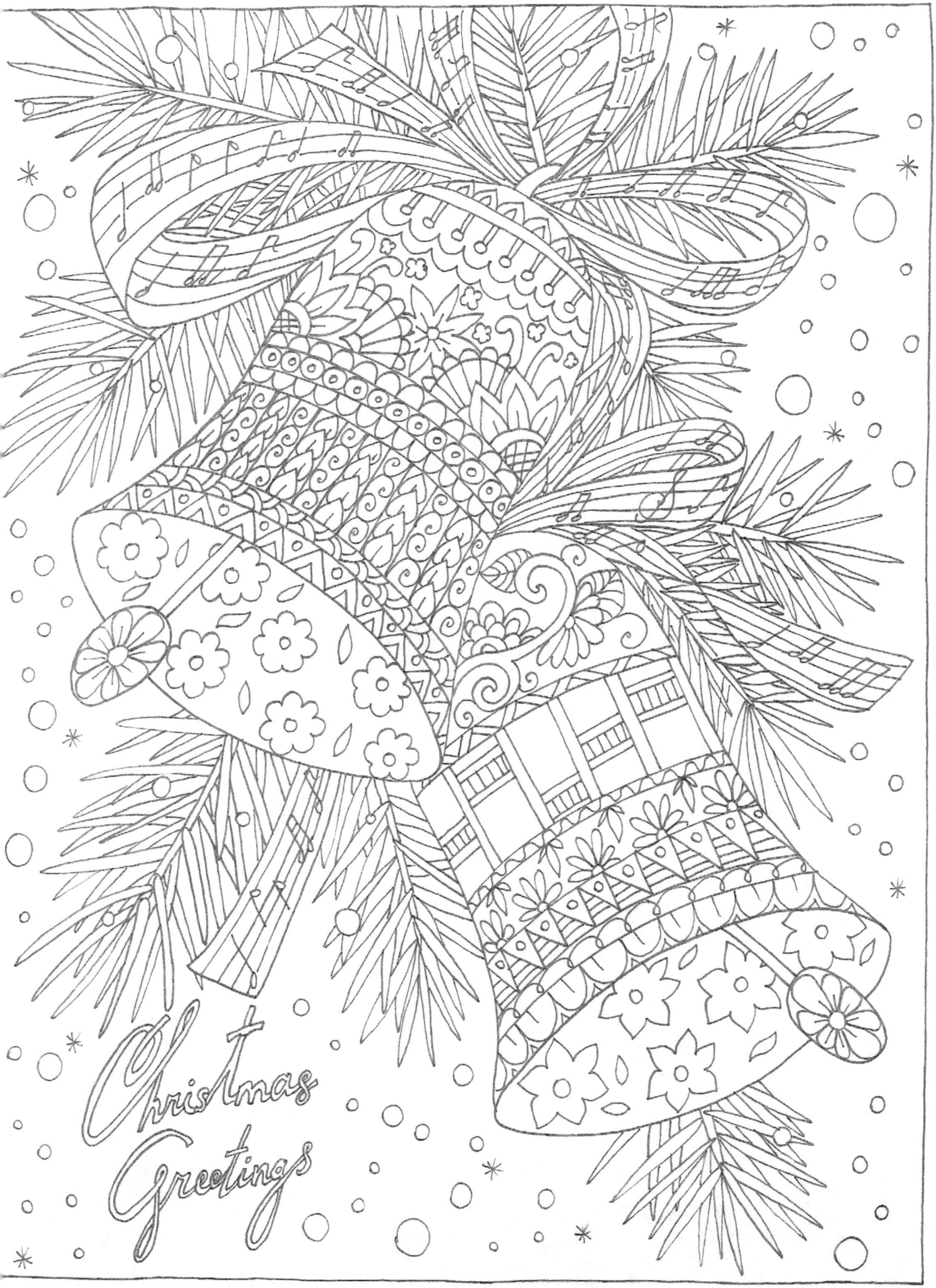
Christmas
Greetings

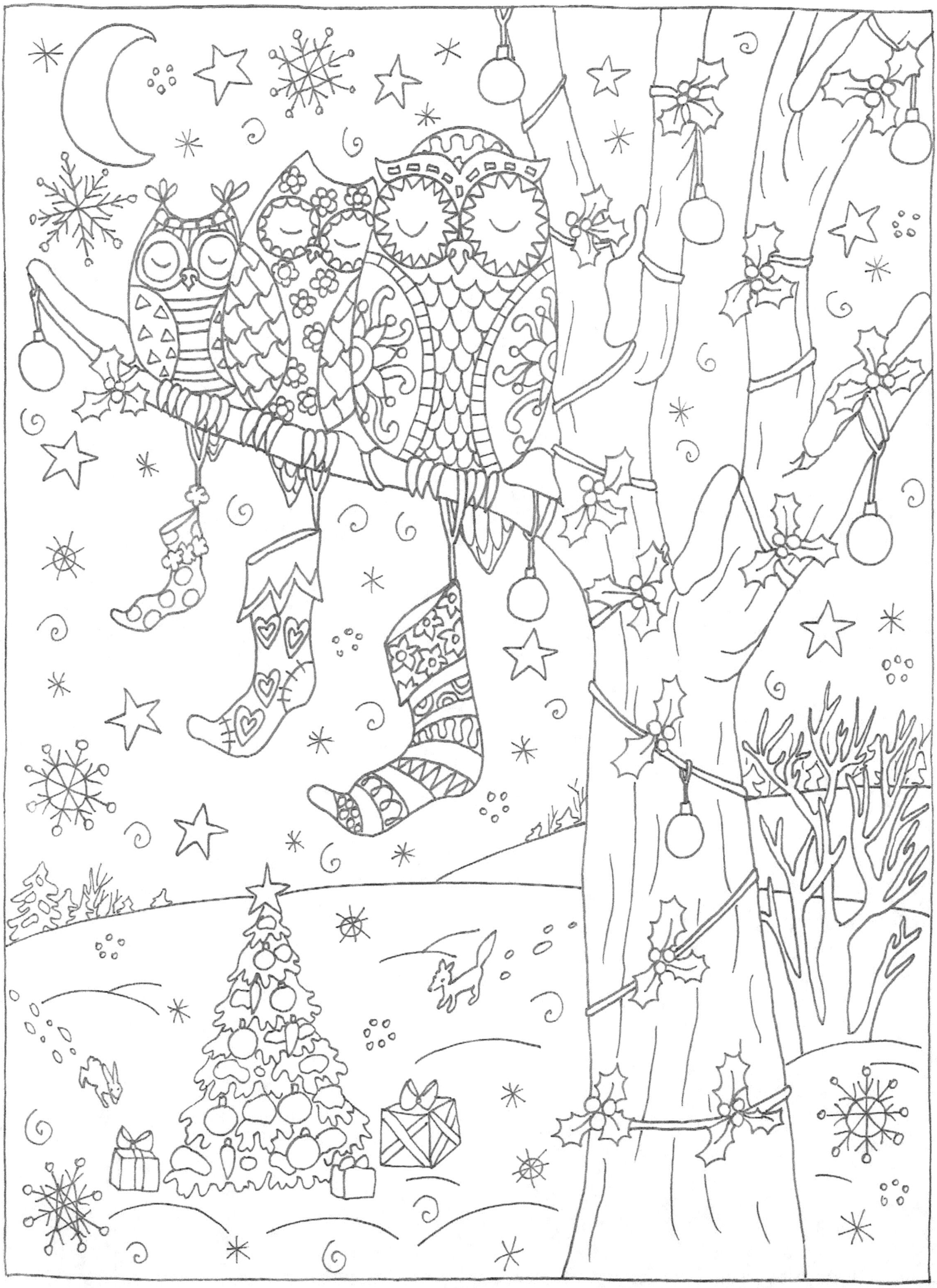

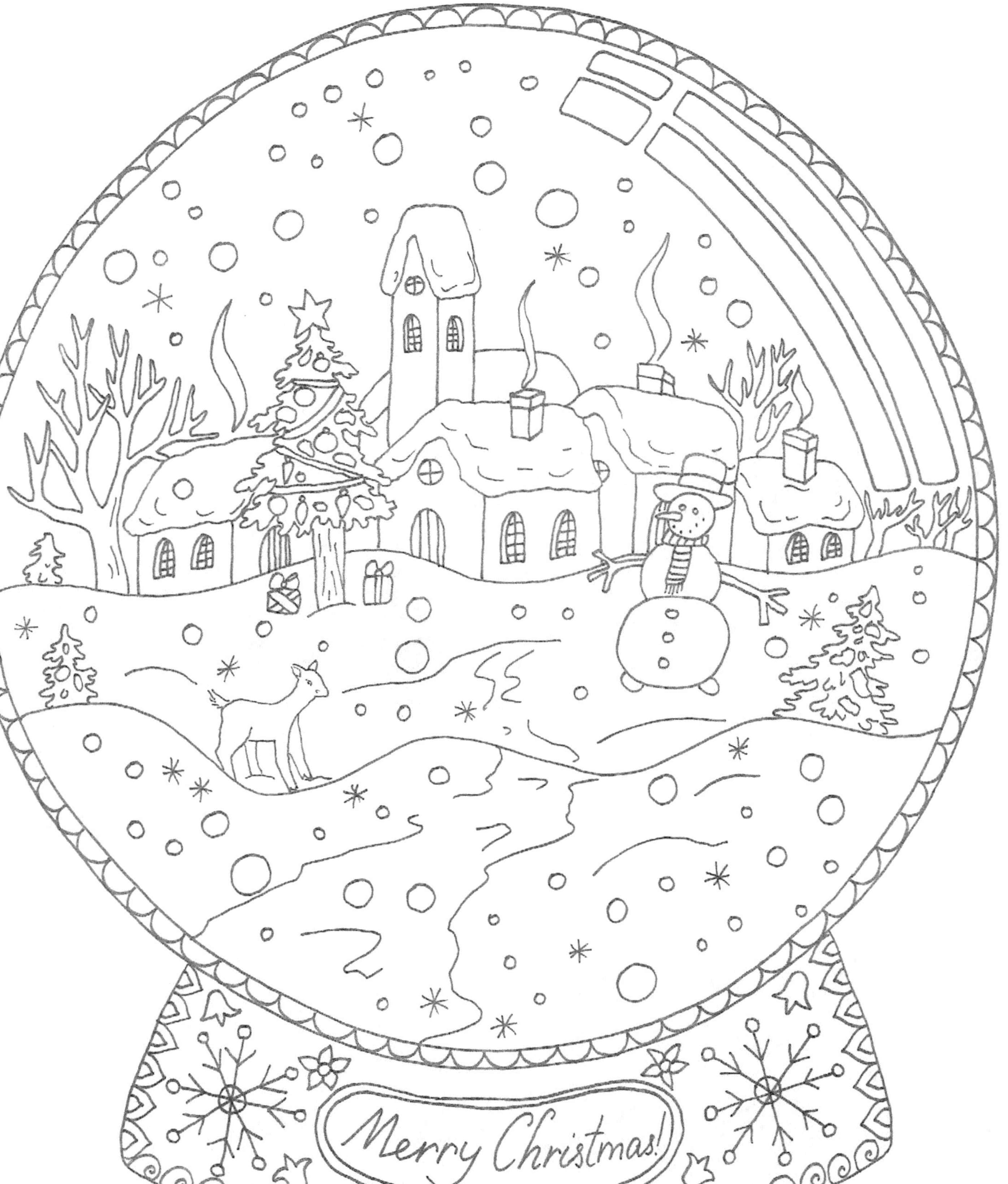
Merry Christmas!

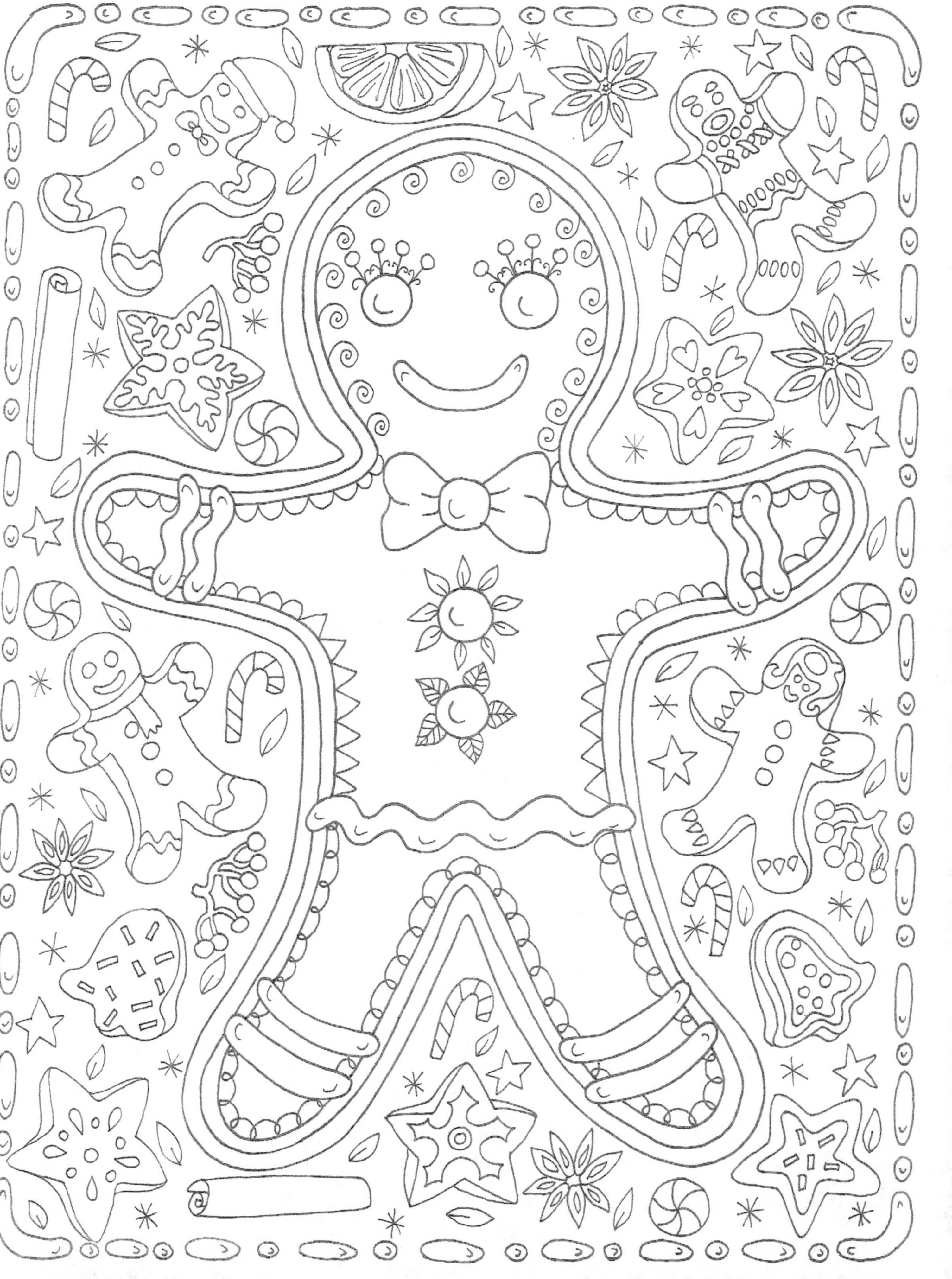

www.ingramcontent.com/pod-product-compliance
Lightning Source LLC
Chambersburg PA
CBHW081302180526
45170CB00007B/2528
* 9 7 8 1 5 4 0 3 1 6 2 9 5 *